ntents

Learning to talk

It's really important that children learn to talk and listen so they can communicate with people around them, learn, make friends and have fun.

When learning to talk, some children will be a little quicker to talk, others will be a little slower. But all should have reached certain stages at certain times.

Babies listen and can recognise voices before they're born. From birth, they learn to communicate by looking at their parents, listening and taking turns. As they develop they begin to understand what people are saying, they learn how to say words and sentences and their speech becomes clear.

But learning to talk doesn't happen by accident, it needs you to make this happen.

Parents are the best people to help their children learn – they know them best, they care about them most and want to give them the best start in life. The more you know, the more you can help.

Helping your child learn to talk can be as easy as you talking, listening and playing with them whenever you can. Lots of children struggle to develop their communication skills – if you know what to expect, you can make sure your child is on the right track.

Check out the information in this guide to find out what helps children learn to talk and listen and to see if your child is on the right track.

If you're worried about your child's talking, use the checklist on page 52 to help explain your concerns to your GP or health visitor, or you can talk directly to your local speech and language therapy department.

Hello world!

Babies start communicating from day one. They communicate by watching your face and making noises. They might even try to copy what you do. Try sticking your tongue out at a baby and see what they do. Being able to copy is important for babies – it's how they learn.

By **6** months...

..babies will usually

- make sounds like cooing, gurgling and babbling, to themselves and with other people
- make noises to get your attention
- watch your face when you talk to them
- get excited when they hear voices, maybe by kicking or waving arms or making noises
- smile and laugh when other people smile and laugh
- make sounds back when someone talks to them

How's your baby doing?

Talk

Copy sounds your baby makes

Can they look at you and maybe even join in?
Can you hear your baby cooing and gurgling to themselves?

Listen

Talk to your baby about what you're doing

Do they watch your face while you're talking?

Take part

Spend time talking and playing with your baby – get down on
the floor to play, talk and listen

Can they join in, smile and laugh with you?

Things to do...

- Talk to your baby. Tell them what you're doing, where you're going and what you notice about them – they're listening and taking it all in

- Sing songs and rhymes, especially those with actions or lots of repetition

- Look at and talk about picture books – it's never too early to share books

For other ideas and games to play visit
www.thecommunicationtrust.org.uk/smalltalk

Getting to know your baby

By the time they're 1, your baby will be communicating with you in more ways – making noises, pointing and looking to get your attention. They'll want to have baby conversations with you and will start to understand routines, simple words and activities.

By 1 year...

...babies will usually

- make talking noises, babble strings of sounds like '**ma-ma-ma**' and '**ba-ba-ba**'. They'll also point and look at you to get your attention

- say their first words and maybe use gestures – though not all 1 year olds will be able to do this

- start to understand words like '**bye-bye**' and '**up**', especially when you use a gesture at the same time

- know the names of familiar objects, such as '**car**', '**daddy**' and '**teddy**'

- take turns in conversations, babbling back to an adult

Talk

Watch your baby
Do they try and get your attention?

What if they want something they can't reach ...
Will they shout, point or make noises?

Listen

Have three or four familiar objects near your baby and ask for one of them - hold out your hand and say "Where's teddy?"
Do they look at the object or point to it? They may even give it to you

Take part

Talk to your baby and leave a space for them to answer
Do they make talking noises and join in the conversation?

Things to do...

- Copy your baby when they're babbling, take turns and 'have a conversation'

- Use actions with words. Try waving as you say **"bye-bye"** or holding your hands out to your baby and saying **"up"** – this will help them understand the words

- Sing action songs like **Incy Wincy Spider** and play games like **Peek-a-Boo** to encourage communication skills

For other ideas and games to play visit
www.thecommunicationtrust.org.uk/smalltalk

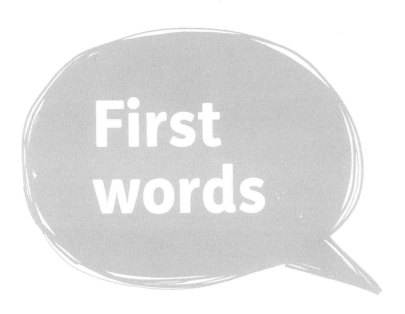

First words

By 18 months, your baby will be starting to talk - this is a very exciting time. Not everyone will understand them but they're making a good try at saying a handful of words.

By **18** months...

...babies will usually

- be talking! They'll be able to say around 20 words. These are usually things you say a lot at home such as **'milk'**, **'daddy'**, **'meow'**, **'hurrah'**, **'bye-bye'**, and **'more'**

- use words in a baby way, not always clearly – strangers or relatives might not understand, but you usually do

- understand some simple words and short phrases. These are usually things they hear a lot in the day, such as **'coat on'**, **'drink'**, **'shoes'**, **'bus'**, **'dinner time'**, and **'all gone'**

- be able to point to familiar objects when you ask them

- be enjoying games like **Peek-a-Boo** and **Pat-a-Cake**

> ## How's **your** baby doing?

Talk

Listen out for what your baby is saying
Can they say words now? How many words do they say?
You could write them down

Listen

Think about something your baby loves to do
Do they get excited when you mention them?
"Dinner time", "Bath time", "Mummy's home"

Take part

Talk and play simple games with your baby – like talk on a pretend phone or build a tower with bricks
Will they explore toys, press buttons, and make noises?
Do they enjoy your company? Do they like playing and exploring?

Things to do...

- If your child is pointing at something, tell them what it is – **"It's a worm!"**

- Sharing books and looking at family photos is a great way of starting conversations with your baby

- Spend time outside together talking, listening and exploring – there's so much to talk about

For other ideas and games to play visit
www.thecommunicationtrust.org.uk/smalltalk

Toddler talk

At 2 years old, your baby is now a toddler and will be exploring the world around them. Their understanding of words and phrases grows really quickly during this time. This can result in frustration when they can't get their message across.

By 2 years...

...toddlers will usually

- use 50 or more single words, like 'juice', 'car, 'biscuit', 'mummy', 'swing', and 'ball'

- start to put short sentences together with two to three words, such as **'more juice'**, **'bye-bye daddy'**, and **'my car'**

- ask simple questions such as **"What that?"** or **"Who that?"** They might do this quite a lot!

- understand between 200 and 500 words

- understand simple questions and instructions, such as **"Where's baby?"**, or **"Go and get your pyjamas"**

- enjoy pretend play with their toys, such as feeding dolly or pretending to drive a car, usually making noises and talking whilst playing

Talk

Play with your toddler and listen out for what they're saying
Are they saying more and more words and putting 2 or 3 words together?

Listen

Can they understand simple questions?
When putting the shopping away say "Find me the apples"
When you're looking at photos can they spot family members if asked?

Take part

Watch how your toddler plays and reacts to others
Do they let you join in with their games? Do they enjoy pretend games with cars or trains, shopping or cooking? Do they enjoy posting shapes and simple puzzles?

Things to do...

- Say and sing action rhymes and songs. This will help toddlers become familiar with the rhythms of language and makes talking and listening active and fun

- Share books together. Books with flaps and different textures are great – take time looking at the pictures and describing them

- Repeat and expand on what your child says. If your child says **"juice"**, you can say **"more juice"**, **"juice please"** or **"juice gone"**. This shows your child how words can be put together to make short sentences

For other ideas and games to play visit
www.thecommunicationtrust.org.uk/smalltalk

Child's talk

By 3 years old, your child will be saying lots more words and talking in longer sentences. This is a really exciting time and children will be asking lots of questions to help them learn and find out about the world around them. They're often keen to have conversations with adults they know well.

By 3 years...

...children will usually

- use different types of words to do different things. For example, to describe: what things look like (**'big'**, **'soft'**), where things are (**'under'**, **'on'**), what things are for (**'eating'**, **'playing'**), how many (**'lots'**), who they are (**'me'**)

- put 4 or 5 words together, such as **"Me a big girl now"**

- have clearer speech, although will still have some baby talk such as **'pider'** instead of **'spider'**

- understand simple **'who'**, **'what'**, and **'where'** questions

- play imaginative games that are longer or have more complicated ideas

- be able to have proper conversations

- listen to and remember simple stories

How's **your** child doing?

Talk

Children are pretty chatty at this age. You should notice that your child can speak in sentences

Can they use words and sentences to ask questions or get what they want? Is their speech so clear that you can understand most of what they say?

Listen

Your 3 year old understands a lot more of what is being said now

Can they remember longer instructions and information? "Teddy is on the sofa", "Find a big plate" or "Draw a house with a red door"

Take part

3 year olds often enjoy the company of adults and other children

Do they watch other children playing and, when they feel comfortable, join in?

33

Things to do...

- Share books and talk about the story and characters. Comment on what the different characters look like and what they do

- If children say words that aren't clear, the best way to help is for you to repeat what they've said using the right words rather than to make them say it again

- To help show your child how to listen, stop for a minute and listen out for what you can hear. You can do this at home or when out and about

For other ideas and games to play visit
www.thecommunicationtrust.org.uk/smalltalk

Little
chatterbox

Your 4 year old should have lots of words and sentences. You can see them using their talking to make new friends or to work out problems. They talk to find out new information, by asking lots of questions. A massive amount of learning happens at this time.

By 4 years...

...children will usually

- ask lots of questions like 'what', 'where' and 'why'

- answer questions about 'why' something has happened, such as "Why are you crying?", "Because I hurted my knee"

- use longer sentences and link sentences together, such as "I had pizza for tea <u>and</u> then I played in the garden"

- describe events that have already happened, such as "We got dressed up and we went to the hall and singed songs. All the mummies and daddies did watch"

- start to like simple jokes, though often their jokes make little sense

- start to be able to plan games with others

- have fluent and mostly clear speech, though will continue to have difficulties with a small number of sounds – such as **'r'** as in **'rabbit'**, **'l'** as in **'letter'**, **'th'** as in **'thumb'**, **'sh'** as in **'show'** or **'j'** as in **'jam'**

- listen to longer stories and answer questions about a story they've just heard. For example, simple questions such as **"Who did Cinderella dance with at the ball?"**, **"Were Cinderella's sisters kind?"**

- understand and often use words that describe colour, number and time, such as **'blue car'**, **'three fingers'** and **'tomorrow is my birthday'**

- enjoy make-believe play

Talk

By 4 years, children can explain their ideas, talk in sentences and talk about things that have happened

Can they explain to someone else an event or activity - where you went and what happened?

Child: "Mum and me and Jasper go park, but he runned away"
Adult: "Oh no, what happened to him?"
Child: "A lady finded him in the cafe - that was lucky wasn't it mummy?"

Listen

Are they able to follow simple two part instructions reasonably well? "Go get your slippers, they're upstairs under mummy's bed"

Are they able to understand questions starting with 'why'? "Why were the three pigs scared of the big bad wolf?"

Take part

Do you hear your child using language to do this?

You might hear them saying things like "Let's pretend we're in a jungle, you be the tiger and I'll be the lion and then..."

Things to do...

- Have a special time to talk about the day. One good way to do this is to say **"Tell me one thing you enjoyed doing today?"**

- Play around with words and sounds – think of words that begin with the same sound or words that rhyme. Rhyming is an important skill when learning to read

- Play quizzes with each other. Describe a character they know and see if they can guess who it is. Then give them a turn to describe and you guess

For other ideas and games to play visit
www.thecommunicationtrust.org.uk/smalltalk

Growing up

At 5 years old your child will be at school. They need to learn how to listen, understand more and share their ideas with new adults and in bigger groups. They also still need to have conversations – to share information, to make friends and explain how they're feeling.

By **5** years...

...children will usually

- take turns in much longer conversations
- use sentences that are well formed, such as "I had spaghetti for tea at Jamilia's house"
- be learning more words all the time and thinking more about what different words mean
- be able to re-tell short stories they've heard in roughly the right order and using language that makes it sound like a story, like "Once upon a time..."
- have fluent speech and use most speech sounds. They may still have trouble with more difficult words such as 'scribble' or 'elephant'. Some speech sounds such as 'r' and 'th' may still be difficult

- enjoy listening to stories, songs and rhymes and they'll start to make up their own

- ask questions or make comments that make sense in relation to what they've heard

- understand spoken instructions while they're doing something else, so they don't have to stop doing other things in order to listen

- understand more complicated language such as 'last', 'might', 'maybe', and 'above'

- use talk to mix with other children and adults, to work things out with others and to have longer conversations

How's **your** child doing?

Talk

Can your child have good conversations? When having a conversation with your child...

Can they organise their thoughts and put longer sentences together?

Can you usually follow what they're saying?

Watch out for...

Do they often get frustrated or give up trying to tell you something? Do they regularly forget words or miss out information? Do they sound muddled and disorganised in their talking? If so, they may be struggling

Listen

Check out how well your child understands

Can they listen to you while they're busy doing something else?

While they're drawing a picture or playing (not watching TV as this is too absorbing), ask them to get their coat and shoes

Are they beginning to get the idea that things can happen at different times?

"Christmas is coming soon - just 5 more sleeps" or by using words like 'morning', 'tomorrow', 'Wednesday'

Watch out for...

If you need to repeat things lots of times or you need to make instructions much simpler, they may be struggling

Take part

Do they talk with other children and join in with group conversations and games?

Check it out by talking to your child about the best thing they did today - these conversations often include different games or activities they play with friends

Things to do...

- Although children may know lots of different words, it's important to introduce new words and phrases. This helps them to continue learning. See if you can think of lots of different words that mean a similar thing – for example different words that mean **'big'**

- Your child may need time to think before responding to questions and instructions. Give them time without answering for them or finishing their sentences

- Playing board games helps children to listen and take turns – both are essential for good conversations

For other ideas and games to play visit
www.thecommunicationtrust.org.uk/smalltalk

Quick look...

This table is a quick reminder of the basics children should be doing at each age - what they should be saying and understanding and how they should be taking part and interacting with others.

	6 months	1 Year	18 months
Talk	Making noises	Making talking noises and often saying their first words	Saying words like "daddy"
Listen	Watching your face when you talk	Understanding simple words like "bye bye"	Understanding simple phrases such as "all gone"
Take part	Smiling when you laugh	Taking turns in 'conversations' with babbling noises	Exploring and enjoying games like Peek-a-Boo

2 years	3 years	4 years	5 years
Putting words together such as "bye bye mummy"	Putting 4 or 5 words together like "my daddy play football"	Asking lots of questions such as "why..."	Talking in more adult like sentences
Understanding simple questions like "Where's baby?"	Listening and remembering simple stories with pictures	Understanding questions about a story "Who climbed the beanstalk?"	Understanding long and more complicated information like "first...and then..."
Enjoying pretending like talking on the phone	Enjoying having proper conversations	Planning more complicated games with others	Taking lots of turns in conversations

Checklist

If you're not sure whether your child's communication skills are on track, use the following pages to highlight the areas you're concerned about.

Remember to check back to the information in this guide on what your child should be doing for their age.

Talk

	✓
They don't have as many words as other children of their age	

notes...

They use shorter sentences than they should for their age	

notes...

They sound muddled when they're talking and difficult to follow	

notes...

Their speech is unclear; they miss out sounds from words or use the wrong sounds, e.g. "a tup of toffee" (a cup of coffee)	

notes...

They struggle to get their words out – it sounds like a stammer	

notes...

Listen

They don't seem to hear or find it difficult to listen for their age

notes...

They can't follow instructions for their age

notes...

They need to hear things lots of times before they understand

notes...

They don't answer questions or when they do, give the wrong answers

notes...

They don't seem to learn new words very easily

notes...

Take part

They don't look at you properly when talking

notes...

They don't seem to listen well

notes...

They don't seem to know how to have a conversation

notes...

They struggle to talk and listen with other children

notes...

They struggle to join in with other children's play or conversations

notes...

Additional information

Children with speech, language and communication needs

Around 10% of all children have long term speech, language and communication needs. Many more have delayed speech, language and communication, where their skills are developing more slowly than expected. These children may have difficulties with:

Speech sounds – they may not be able to say the right sounds in words or they may miss out some sounds altogether, which means their speech is unclear. For example, "a tup of tea"

Fluency – they might have a stammer. They may have a lot of hesitations in their speech and repeat sounds, words or sentences and sometimes they may struggle to get words out altogether

Understanding of language – they may struggle to understand words and sentences

Spoken language (talking) – they may not use many words or be able to put words together to make sentences or may be very muddled and disorganised when trying to talk

Social use of language – they might use lots of words and can put sentences together, but don't know how to use their language to have conversations, play or make friends with other children well

Children with speech, language and communication needs can have one or any combination of the above. For more information see the publication *Misunderstood*, available to download and order for free at www.hello.org.uk/resources

If your child's first language isn't English

Speaking more than one language can have many positive benefits. When your child is learning to talk and understand, it's important to talk to them in the language you feel most confident in.

Children learn to talk through listening and talking to people – it's the same for their first language and English.

If you feel your child is struggling in their first language, as well as English, it would be a good idea to talk to your GP, health visitor or local speech and language therapy department. You can use the checklist on page 54 to help you explain your concerns.

For further information

www.talkingpoint.org.uk

Talking Point is a website all about children's speech, language and communication. It's designed for parents, people that work with children and children and young people themselves.

It contains everything you need to know about supporting children's speech and language development. Talking Point helps you to identify if a child is struggling and it tells you what to do.

The site contains valuable resources which can be downloaded for free and used to support children as well as links to lots of other places that can help. Talking Point is run by I CAN and funded by *Hello* - the national year of communication.

If you're worried about your child's communication development you can talk directly to a speech and language therapist, who is an expert in children's communication.

The Talking Point website has a database of local support services including speech and language therapy departments. You can search for your local services at **www.talkingpoint.org.uk/talkinglinks**, simply type in your post code.

About The Communication Trust

The Communication Trust is a group of nearly 50 voluntary sector organisations, bringing together their expertise to ensure that the speech, language and communication needs of all children and young people are met. We do this by signposting specialist training, support and guidance to people working with children. The Trust was founded by children's charities Afasic and I CAN together with BT and the Council for Disabled Children.

To find out more about The Communication Trust please go to www.thecommunicationtrust.org.uk

To find out more about the organisations involved with The Communication Trust who support children who have communication needs and their families please go to: www.thecommunicationtrust.org.uk/partners

The Communication Trust
Every child understood

About *Hello*

During 2011 The Communication Trust ran the *Hello* campaign, which was the 2011 national year of communication. The campaign aimed to increase understanding of how important it is for all children and young people to develop good communication skills.

It's estimated that over 1 million UK children have some form of speech, language and communication need that requires them to have extra help to communicate. This can affect them severely and for life.

To find out more about Hello, including accessing the resources that were developed, please visit www.thecommunicationtrust.org.uk/hello to find out more about the campaign and sign up for regular updates.

Hello was managed in partnership with the Office of the Communication Champion

Written by Wendy Lee, Professional Director, The Communication Trust.

Thank you to those who made additional contributions to this publication.

To order further copies of this booklet please go to
www.thecommunicationtrust.org.uk/smalltalk

Designed by:
The Design Conspiracy - www.thedesignconspiracy.com

Illustrations by:
Nila Aye (©Nila Aye 2011) - www.nilaaye.com

Second edition, published August 2012. ©The Communication Trust

First published May 2011. This edition was supported by BT for Hello,
the national year of communication,
www.thecommunicationtrust.org.uk/hello

To find out more about BT's resources please go to
www.bt.com/learningskills